Table of Contents

Acknowledgments

"This book is the result of a unique collaboration between human creativity and artificial intelligence. We want to thank every curious mind exploring AI and everyone who has contributed to advancing its development. Special thanks to our readers for embracing this journey into understanding how machines and humans are shaping the future together."

Foreword

"What happens when an artificial intelligence and a human team up to write a book? The result is not just a guide to AI, but a reflection of the possibilities when humans and machines work together."

This book was written with a unique approach: an AI as the primary writer, and a human as the guide. Through this collaboration, we aim to introduce AI in an accessible way—demystifying its workings, addressing its potential, and highlighting its role in shaping our future.

Whether you're new to AI or simply curious about how it impacts your life, this book is for you. With stories, insights, and practical examples, we explore the unfolding relationship between humans and machines.

Welcome to the journey.

Theme 1: The Origins of Intelligence

"To create intelligence, we first had to understand it."

Every revolutionary idea starts with a question. For AI, the question was simple yet profound: *Can a machine think?* Answering this sparked decades of exploration, experimentation, and breakthroughs. This theme takes us back to the origins of artificial intelligence, the brilliant minds that shaped it, and the early steps that transformed AI from an idea into reality.

1. The Philosophical Roots: What Does It Mean to Think?

Long before machines, philosophers wrestled with the concept of intelligence.

- In **1637**, René Descartes famously declared, *"I think, therefore I am,"* linking thought to existence.
- **19th-century visionaries**, like Ada Lovelace, speculated about machines capable of "thinking" beyond calculation, imagining a future where machines could compose music or analyze data creatively.

These early ideas planted the seeds of artificial intelligence—a vision that machines might one day replicate the complexities of the human mind.

2. Alan Turing: The Father of Modern AI

The journey truly began with **Alan Turing**, a British mathematician whose ideas bridged philosophy and computation.

Turing's Breakthroughs

- During World War II, Turing led the development of the **Enigma machine**, a device that deciphered Nazi codes. This success proved machines could solve complex problems faster than humans.
- In **1950**, Turing published his seminal paper *"Computing Machinery and Intelligence,"* asking: *"Can machines think?"*
  - He proposed the **Turing Test**: if a machine's responses could fool a human into thinking it was human, it could be considered intelligent.

Why It Mattered

Turing's ideas weren't just technical—they were deeply philosophical. He saw machines as tools to expand human potential, not replace it.

3. The Dartmouth Conference: AI is Born

In **1956**, a group of ambitious researchers gathered at Dartmouth College to answer a bold question: *"How can we make machines intelligent?"*

John McCarthy and the Birth of AI

- John McCarthy, a young computer scientist, coined the term **"Artificial Intelligence"** during this conference.
- The group believed machines could mimic human reasoning, learning, and decision-making through mathematical models.

Early Breakthroughs

- **Logic Theorist (1956)**: The first AI program, created by Allen Newell and Herbert Simon, could prove mathematical theorems.
- **Chess Programs**: Early AI systems like IBM's chess-playing programs demonstrated machines could handle strategic thinking.

Why It Mattered

The Dartmouth Conference marked the birth of AI as a formal field of study, setting a vision for decades of exploration.

4. The Early Visionaries

Beyond Turing and McCarthy, countless pioneers contributed to AI's foundation:

- **Marvin Minsky**: Known as the "architect of AI," Minsky envisioned machines with human-like intelligence and founded MIT's AI lab.
- **Frank Rosenblatt**: Developed the **Perceptron** in 1958, an early neural network model inspired by the human brain.

- **Arthur Samuel**: Created a checkers-playing program that could learn and improve over time, showcasing **machine learning** in action.

Each of these individuals brought AI closer to reality, laying the groundwork for modern breakthroughs.

5. The First AI Winter: Dreams on Pause

Despite early successes, AI hit a major roadblock in the 1970s. Funding dried up as progress slowed, and critics dismissed AI as overhyped.

The Problem

- Early AI systems relied heavily on rules and lacked the flexibility of human intelligence.
- Computers were too slow, and data was limited, making it impossible to tackle real-world problems.

The Revival

AI wouldn't stay dormant for long. The rise of **expert systems** in the 1980s—software that mimicked human decision-making in specific domains—brought renewed optimism.

6. The Rise of Machine Learning

AI's second chapter began with the realization that machines could learn from data.

Game-Changing Ideas

- **1986**: Geoffrey Hinton introduced the concept of **backpropagation**, a method for training neural networks.
- **1997**: IBM's **Deep Blue** defeated Garry Kasparov, the reigning chess world champion. For the first time, a machine mastered complex human strategy.

Why It Mattered

These breakthroughs showed that AI wasn't just about rules—it was about learning, adaptation, and creativity.

7. Case Study: Deep Blue vs. Kasparov

In 1997, IBM's Deep Blue became the first machine to defeat a world chess champion, Garry Kasparov, in a six-game match.

What Made Deep Blue Special?

- It could calculate 200 million possible moves per second.
- Unlike human players, it never got tired or emotional.

The Human Reaction

While some hailed this as a victory for technology, others worried it marked the beginning of machines surpassing humans. Kasparov himself described the experience as "humbling."

Legacy

Deep Blue wasn't "intelligent" in the human sense, but it showed the potential of AI to handle complexity at an unmatched scale.

8. Why the Origins of AI Matter Today

Understanding where AI came from helps us see where it's headed.

- Early pioneers like Turing and McCarthy didn't just build machines—they imagined possibilities.
- Every AI system today, from ChatGPT to self-driving cars, stands on the shoulders of these visionaries.

Key Takeaway

AI's origins remind us that innovation is a human endeavor, driven by curiosity, creativity, and the desire to solve problems.

"The story of AI's beginnings isn't just about technology—it's about humanity's determination to understand intelligence itself. As we explore what AI means today, let's remember the visionaries who made it all possible."

Theme 2: AI in Everyday Life

"If you think AI is futuristic, think again—it's already shaping your daily life in ways you may not realize."

Artificial Intelligence isn't just in labs or high-tech industries; it's in your pocket, your home, and the services you use every day. This theme uncovers how AI powers the tools we rely on, making life more convenient, efficient, and connected.

1. AI in Your Pocket: Smartphones

1.1 Virtual Assistants

Your smartphone is likely home to a virtual assistant like Siri, Google Assistant, or Alexa.

- **What It Does**: These AI systems understand your voice, process your commands, and provide answers or actions.
- **How It Works**: AI uses natural language processing (NLP) to convert speech into data it can analyze.

Example:
"Hey Google, what's the weather today?" In seconds, AI analyzes your location, accesses weather data, and delivers a human-like response.

1.2 Predictive Text and Autocorrect

Every time you type, AI predicts what you're going to say or fixes typos based on learned language patterns.

- **Example**: Autocorrect systems have learned to adapt to slang and even emojis, making them more user-friendly.

2. AI at Home: Smart Devices

AI isn't limited to your phone—it's embedded in everyday devices that make your home smarter.

2.1 Smart Thermostats (e.g., Nest)

- **What It Does**: Learns your temperature preferences and adjusts automatically.
- **Why It Matters**: Saves energy and keeps you comfortable without manual adjustments.

2.2 Robot Vacuums (e.g., Roomba)

- **What It Does**: Maps your home, avoids obstacles, and cleans efficiently.
- **How It Works**: AI uses sensors and algorithms to navigate spaces intelligently.

2.3 Smart Speakers

- **Example**: Amazon Echo or Google Home goes beyond playing music. It controls your lights, orders groceries, and even answers trivia questions.

3. AI in Entertainment

AI has transformed how we consume content, making experiences more personalized than ever.

3.1 Streaming Services (Netflix, Spotify, YouTube)

- **What It Does**: Analyzes your preferences and recommends content tailored to your tastes.
- **How It Works**: AI compares your habits with millions of other users to predict what you'll enjoy.

Case Study: Netflix's Recommendation Engine

- Netflix uses AI to analyze watch history, pause points, and user ratings.
- The result? 80% of streamed content on Netflix is driven by AI recommendations.

3.2 Gaming

- AI enhances gaming experiences by creating intelligent opponents (NPCs) and personalizing gameplay.
- **Example**: OpenAI's Dota 2 bot team defeated world-class players, showcasing AI's ability to master complex strategies.

4. AI in Your Daily Errands

4.1 Online Shopping (Amazon, eBay)

- **What It Does**: Recommends products based on your browsing and purchase history.

- **How It Works**: AI identifies patterns in your behavior to suggest what you're most likely to buy.

4.2 Navigation (Google Maps, Waze)

- **What It Does**: Suggests the fastest routes based on real-time traffic data.
- **How It Works**: AI processes millions of data points from drivers to predict traffic and delays.

Case Study: Google Maps' Traffic Predictions

- Google Maps uses anonymized data from smartphones to estimate traffic congestion.
- It combines historical patterns with live updates to reroute drivers efficiently.

5. AI in Work and Productivity

5.1 Email Filters (Gmail)

- AI automatically separates important emails from spam using machine learning.
- **Impact**: Saves time and improves productivity for millions of users daily.

5.2 Virtual Meeting Transcriptions (Zoom, Otter.ai)

- AI generates real-time captions, making meetings accessible and easier to review.

5.3 Task Automation

- Tools like Zapier and IFTTT use AI to automate repetitive tasks, from scheduling to sending reminders.

6. AI in Health and Fitness

6.1 Wearable Devices (Fitbit, Apple Watch)

- **What It Does**: Tracks steps, heart rate, and sleep patterns, offering personalized health insights.
- **How It Works**: AI analyzes your activity data to provide actionable recommendations.

6.2 Fitness Apps (MyFitnessPal, Strava)

- **Example**: MyFitnessPal uses AI to analyze eating habits and suggest healthier choices.

7. AI on Social Media

7.1 Content Recommendations

- Platforms like Instagram and TikTok use AI to personalize your feed based on your behavior.
- **Impact**: Keeps users engaged by showing content they're most likely to interact with.

7.2 Photo Tagging

- **Example**: Facebook automatically tags your friends in photos using facial recognition AI.

8. Balancing Convenience and Concerns

While AI makes life easier, it also raises important questions:

- **Privacy**: AI systems collect and analyze vast amounts of personal data.
  - **Example**: Smart speakers like Alexa listen to your commands—but how much are they really listening?
- **Over-Personalization**: AI can create "filter bubbles," exposing you only to content that reinforces your existing views.

Key Takeaway: The benefits of AI in everyday life are undeniable, but understanding how it works helps you use it responsibly.

9. Why It Matters

AI isn't just a background tool—it's a partner in your daily routines. Knowing how AI powers the tools you use helps you make informed decisions and appreciate its role in making life simpler.

"AI is no longer a futuristic concept. It's here, enhancing our lives in ways both big and small. By understanding its role, we can harness its power while staying aware of its challenges."

Theme 3: Learning Like a Machine

"To teach machines to think, we first had to teach them to learn."

AI doesn't wake up one day knowing how to drive a car or write a poem. It learns, much like humans do—but with key differences. This theme explains how machines process data, learn patterns, and improve over time, turning raw information into intelligent decisions.

1. How AI Learns: A Simple Analogy

Imagine teaching a child to recognize a dog:

- You show them pictures of different dogs.
- You point out key features—ears, tails, fur.
- Over time, the child learns to identify dogs on their own.

AI works in a similar way, except it learns from **data** instead of experience. The process can be broken into three main steps:

1. **Input Data**: Examples (like dog photos) are fed into the AI system.
2. **Pattern Recognition**: The system identifies common features in the data.
3. **Decision Making**: It applies what it has learned to new, unseen examples.

2. Types of Machine Learning

AI systems use different methods to learn, depending on the task. Here are the three main types:

2.1 Supervised Learning: Learning with a Teacher

- **What It Is**: The AI is given labeled data and learns by example.
- **Example**: Feeding the AI thousands of photos labeled "cat" or "dog" to teach it to classify animals.
- **Real-Life Application**: Spam filters in email systems. The AI is trained on examples of "spam" and "not spam."

2.2 Unsupervised Learning: Discovering Patterns

- **What It Is**: The AI is given unlabeled data and must find patterns on its own.
- **Example**: Grouping customers by shopping habits without being told what the groups mean.
- **Real-Life Application**: Netflix's recommendation system, which clusters users with similar tastes.

2.3 Reinforcement Learning: Trial and Error

- **What It Is**: The AI learns by interacting with its environment and receiving rewards or penalties.
- **Example**: Teaching a robot to navigate a maze by rewarding it for correct moves.
- **Real-Life Application**: Self-driving cars that learn to drive safely by avoiding collisions and following traffic rules.

3. Neural Networks: The Brain of AI

At the heart of AI is the **neural network**, a system inspired by the human brain.

How It Works

- Neural networks are made up of layers of "neurons."
    1. **Input Layer**: Receives raw data (e.g., pixels from an image).
    2. **Hidden Layers**: Processes the data, finding patterns.
    3. **Output Layer**: Produces a result (e.g., "cat" or "dog").

Why It's Powerful

Neural networks can handle complex tasks, like recognizing faces or understanding speech, by analyzing millions of examples.

4. Case Study: AlphaGo and Reinforcement Learning

In 2016, Google's DeepMind created **AlphaGo**, an AI that defeated the world champion in Go, a board game more complex than chess.

How AlphaGo Learned

1. It analyzed millions of past games to understand strategies.

2. It played against itself thousands of times, improving through trial and error.
3. It developed new strategies that even human players hadn't considered.

The Impact

AlphaGo's success wasn't just about winning a game—it showed the potential of reinforcement learning to tackle problems with infinite possibilities.

5. Why Machines Learn Differently

Unlike humans, AI has no intuition or context. It learns purely from data.

Strengths

- AI can process massive amounts of information quickly.
- AI identifies patterns humans might miss.

Weaknesses

- AI struggles with tasks outside its training.
- AI can't understand context or emotion.

Example:
A human knows that a photo of a cat wearing a hat is still a cat. An AI might get confused if it wasn't trained on similar images.

6. The Importance of Data in Learning

AI is only as good as the data it's trained on. Here's why data quality matters:

Bias in Data

If the data is biased, the AI will be too.

- **Example**: A hiring AI trained on past resumes might favor male candidates if the data reflects gender bias.

The Need for Diversity

Training AI on diverse data ensures it performs well across different scenarios.

Case Study: IBM Watson in Healthcare
IBM's Watson was trained to analyze medical records and assist doctors. However, it struggled with accuracy because the training data wasn't diverse enough to cover rare conditions.

7. How AI Gets Better Over Time

Continuous Learning

Some AI systems improve through feedback.

- **Example**: Google Maps gets better at predicting traffic by analyzing data from millions of drivers every day.

Retraining

AI models are regularly updated with new data to stay relevant.

- **Example**: A weather prediction AI is retrained as climate patterns change.

8. What This Means for You

Understanding how AI learns helps you:

1. **Use AI Effectively**: Knowing its strengths and limitations ensures you get the most out of AI tools.
2. **Spot Bias**: Recognize when AI might be making unfair decisions.
3. **Stay Informed**: Appreciate the role of data in shaping AI's behavior.

"AI's ability to learn is its greatest strength—and its greatest vulnerability. By understanding how machines learn, we can ensure they serve humanity responsibly and effectively."

Theme 4: The Ethics of Intelligence

"With great power comes great responsibility."

AI is powerful, but power must be accompanied by ethical principles. Without proper oversight, AI can lead to unintended consequences like unfair decisions or privacy concerns. This theme explores practical ethical challenges in AI development and usage, along with straightforward examples of how to address them.

1. Why Ethics in AI Matters

AI doesn't just process numbers; it impacts lives. Ethical principles are crucial to ensure AI:

- Treats everyone fairly.
- Respects privacy and autonomy.
- Builds trust by being transparent and accountable.

Key Insight: Ethics in AI isn't just about technology—it's about protecting people.

2. Case Study: Automated Loan Approvals

AI is widely used in financial services to determine loan eligibility, but errors in the system can lead to unfair decisions.

The Challenge

- A bank's AI system denied loans to small business owners because it prioritized certain patterns in data (e.g., large urban businesses) without understanding context.
- Many eligible applicants were unfairly rejected.

The Fix

- The bank improved its system by retraining the AI on more diverse data, including businesses from different regions and scales.
- Human oversight was added to review AI decisions before final approvals.

Lesson: AI works best when paired with human judgment.

3. Privacy: Protecting User Data

AI thrives on data, but how do we ensure it doesn't cross boundaries?

Example: Smart Assistants

- Devices like Alexa and Google Assistant record audio snippets to improve their performance.
- However, concerns arose when users realized recordings were sometimes stored and reviewed without consent.

The Solution

- Companies added clear opt-in settings, allowing users to decide whether their data could be stored.
- Transparency was improved through notifications about how data was being used.

Key Insight: User control builds trust in AI systems.

4. Accountability: Who's Responsible for AI?

When AI makes decisions, accountability can become blurred.

- In 2018, a self-driving car involved in testing caused an accident because it failed to identify a pedestrian crossing the road.
- The event raised questions: Was the fault with the car's manufacturer, the software developer, or the safety driver?

The Way Forward

- Clear regulations are needed to define accountability in AI-powered systems.
- Safety standards, similar to those used for airplanes, should be applied to autonomous vehicles.

Lesson: Accountability frameworks are essential for public trust.

5. The Ethical Dilemma of AI Automation

AI automates repetitive tasks, but where do we draw the line between efficiency and over-reliance?

Case Study: Warehouse Robots

- Many warehouses use AI-powered robots to sort, pack, and ship goods.
- While this improves productivity, workers sometimes struggle to keep up with robot-driven workflows, leading to burnout.

The Solution

- Companies adjusted robot pacing to better align with human capabilities.
- AI was repurposed to assist workers rather than push them to the limit.

Key Insight: AI should empower humans, not replace them or create undue stress.

6. Building Ethical AI

How can we ensure AI systems are fair, transparent, and reliable?

1. Diverse Testing Data

- AI systems need to be trained on data that reflects a wide variety of use cases.
- **Example**: A language translation app was retrained using texts from different dialects, improving accuracy across regions.

2. Transparent Decision-Making

- AI should explain its decisions in a way users can understand.
- **Example**: An AI-powered credit scoring system provided users with a clear breakdown of why their score was calculated a certain way.

3. Regular Audits

- AI systems should be reviewed periodically to ensure fairness and accuracy.
- **Example**: A healthcare AI was audited to confirm it was recommending treatments consistently across patients.

7. Why Simplicity in Ethics Matters

Ethical AI doesn't have to be complicated. By focusing on transparency, accountability, and fairness, we can address most concerns and build trust.

Key Takeaway: Simpler solutions—like clear consent options, regular reviews, and open communication—go a long way in making AI trustworthy.

8. The Ethical Imperative: Balancing Innovation with Responsibility

AI's potential is limitless, but ethical considerations must guide its development. By balancing innovation with responsibility, we can ensure AI enhances humanity rather than creating new problems.

"Ethical AI isn't just a technical challenge—it's a human responsibility. By addressing practical concerns with thoughtful solutions, we can ensure AI serves the greater good."

Theme 5: Collaboration, Not Competition

"The future of AI isn't about replacing humans—it's about working alongside us."

Artificial Intelligence is often framed as a competitor, but in reality, it thrives as a collaborator. By combining AI's strengths with human creativity, empathy, and judgment, we unlock new possibilities for innovation, productivity, and problem-solving. This theme highlights real-world examples where humans and AI are working together to achieve remarkable results.

1. Why Collaboration Matters

AI is best at repetitive, data-driven tasks, while humans excel at creativity, empathy, and complex decision-making. Together, they form a partnership where:

- **AI handles the heavy lifting** of data processing and pattern recognition.
- **Humans provide the vision** to direct AI toward meaningful outcomes.

Key Insight: Collaboration between humans and AI amplifies what both can achieve.

2. Case Study: AI in Healthcare

How AI Helps Doctors

- AI-powered tools analyze medical scans, detecting conditions like cancer earlier than traditional methods.
- Example: Google's AI system achieved 99% accuracy in identifying breast cancer in mammograms, acting as a second pair of eyes for radiologists.

How Doctors Enhance AI

- Doctors interpret AI results in the context of patient history, symptoms, and treatment goals.
- Final decisions are always made by humans, ensuring a personalized and ethical approach.

Lesson: AI supports healthcare professionals rather than replacing their expertise.

3. AI as a Creative Partner

- AI tools like OpenAI's DALL·E generate visuals based on text prompts, while systems like AIVA compose original music.
- Human creators use these tools to spark ideas, refine concepts, or explore new creative directions.

Real-World Application

- In advertising, AI suggests campaign ideas based on consumer behavior, but humans shape the message to resonate emotionally.

Key Insight: AI amplifies creativity by removing technical barriers and offering new perspectives.

4. AI in Business: Driving Smarter Decisions

How AI Supports Teams

- AI analyzes large datasets, uncovering trends that would take humans weeks to identify.

- Example: AI-powered sales tools predict customer behavior, helping teams prioritize leads.

How Teams Use AI Insights

- Humans interpret AI findings to develop strategies, build relationships, and adapt to changing markets.

Case Study: Inventory Management

- Retailers use AI to forecast demand and optimize inventory. When combined with human intuition about trends (e.g., holiday shopping habits), businesses achieve higher efficiency and customer satisfaction.

5. Learning from Each Other

AI isn't static—it learns from human interactions, and humans learn how to use AI effectively.

- Tools like Duolingo use AI to adapt lessons to each user's progress, while language learners provide feedback to improve the system.

Key Insight

- AI becomes more effective with human input, while humans grow more skilled by using AI as a learning tool.

6. Case Study: Self-Driving Cars

The AI Role

- AI systems process real-time data from cameras and sensors, making split-second decisions to navigate roads safely.

The Human Role

- Engineers oversee and refine AI algorithms, ensuring they align with safety standards.

- Drivers remain vigilant, ready to take control if needed.

Lesson: Self-driving technology isn't about removing humans—it's about creating a safer driving experience through collaboration.

7. Challenges of Collaboration

1. Over-Reliance on AI

- Relying too heavily on AI can lead to complacency or loss of critical skills.
- **Example**: Pilots must maintain manual flying skills, even with AI autopilot systems.

2. Building Trust

- For collaboration to succeed, humans must trust AI to deliver reliable results.
- **Solution**: Transparent systems that explain how decisions are made build confidence.

8. Why Collaboration is the Future

The best results come when humans and AI work together:

- **Efficiency**: AI handles repetitive tasks, freeing humans for creative and strategic work.
- **Accuracy**: AI reduces errors in data-heavy processes.
- **Innovation**: Humans use AI to explore ideas and solve problems in new ways.

9. What This Means for You

To thrive in an AI-driven world, focus on:

1. **Learning to Use AI Tools**: From chatbots to design software, AI can enhance your skills.
2. **Developing Unique Human Strengths**: Creativity, empathy, and leadership remain irreplaceable.
3. **Embracing AI as a Partner**: View AI as a collaborator that empowers you to do more.

"The future isn't about humans versus machines—it's about humans and machines creating something greater together. Collaboration isn't just the best path forward; it's the only path."

Theme 6: Shaping the Future

"AI is a tool for transformation—but the shape of the future depends on us."

Artificial Intelligence holds the potential to revolutionize industries, solve global problems, and push the boundaries of what humanity can achieve. However, its true impact depends on how we design, deploy, and regulate it. In this theme, we explore AI's possibilities for the future and the responsibility that comes with shaping its direction.

---

1. The Future of AI: What's Possible?

1.1 Healthcare: Saving Lives and Extending Lifespans

- AI-powered diagnostic tools already detect diseases like cancer earlier and more accurately than humans alone.
- **Future Vision**: Personalized medicine tailored to an individual's genetic profile, ensuring treatments with maximum effectiveness and minimal side effects.

Example: AI is being developed to predict diseases before symptoms appear by analyzing subtle changes in a person's health data over time.

1.2 Education: A New Era of Learning

- AI will revolutionize education by adapting lessons to each student's pace and learning style.
- **Future Vision**: Virtual tutors that offer one-on-one learning experiences to students in remote areas, democratizing access to quality education.

Case Study: AI-driven platforms like Khan Academy are already personalizing education for millions of students worldwide.

1.3 Climate and Sustainability

- AI can analyze climate data to predict weather patterns, monitor deforestation, and optimize renewable energy sources.
- **Future Vision**: AI systems coordinating global efforts to combat climate change by managing resources more efficiently.

Example: AI-powered drones are planting trees faster than human efforts, accelerating reforestation initiatives.

2. The Role of Humans in Shaping AI's Future

AI is not a force of nature—it's a human-made tool, and we decide how it evolves.

2.1 Setting Ethical Guidelines

- Governments, organizations, and communities must work together to ensure AI is developed ethically.

Key Insight: Ethical AI starts with clear principles—fairness, transparency, and accountability.

2.2 Bridging the Skills Gap

- As AI changes the job market, reskilling and upskilling initiatives will be critical.
- **Example**: Governments partnering with tech companies to train workers for AI-driven industries.

3. The Challenges of the Future

3.1 Avoiding AI Misuse

- AI can be weaponized in the wrong hands, from autonomous drones to deepfake propaganda.
- **Solution**: Global cooperation to regulate the use of AI in sensitive areas like defense and media.

3.2 Ensuring Accessibility

- If AI benefits are limited to wealthy nations or organizations, it could deepen global inequality.
- **Solution**: Open-source AI tools and affordable AI-powered solutions for developing countries.

4. The Opportunity to Solve Grand Challenges

AI has the potential to address problems once thought unsolvable.

- AI-powered tools predict crop yields, identify disease outbreaks in plants, and optimize irrigation for sustainable farming.
- **Result**: Increased food production in areas struggling with hunger.

Case Study: AI in Disaster Response

- During natural disasters, AI analyzes satellite imagery to identify affected areas and prioritize rescue operations.

Key Insight: AI magnifies human efforts, enabling faster, more effective responses to global crises.

5. Collaboration Across Borders

Why It's Essential

- The challenges AI can address—climate change, pandemics, resource scarcity—don't stop at borders.

- International collaboration ensures AI solutions are scalable and inclusive.

Example: The UN's AI for Good initiative brings together experts from around the world to tackle global challenges.

6. Building the Future Together

1. Transparency and Trust

- AI systems must be transparent about how decisions are made to build public trust.
- **Example**: Healthcare AI explaining why a specific treatment was recommended ensures confidence in its use.

2. Empowering the Next Generation

- Educating young people about AI prepares them to shape its future responsibly.
- **Example**: AI literacy programs in schools teach students how to think critically about technology.

7. Why Shaping AI's Future Matters

What's at Stake

- The future of AI isn't predetermined—it's a reflection of our choices today.
- By prioritizing fairness, accessibility, and sustainability, we can ensure AI serves the greater good.

"The future of AI is not a question of what machines can do—it's a question of what we choose to do with them. Together, we can shape a future where AI amplifies human potential and solves humanity's greatest challenges."

Theme 7: The Human Chapter in AI's Story

"AI is not the protagonist of the future—we are. The story of artificial intelligence is, at its heart, a human story."

Artificial Intelligence is changing the world, but its true power lies in how we choose to use it. From the earliest questions about machine intelligence to today's powerful applications, AI's journey reflects humanity's desire to understand, create, and improve. As this story unfolds, the role we play will determine whether AI becomes a tool for progress or a source of division.

---

1. The Lessons We've Learned

AI is a Tool, Not a Replacement

- AI enhances our abilities but cannot replicate our creativity, empathy, or purpose.

The Importance of Ethics and Responsibility

- Fairness, transparency, and accountability are non-negotiable as AI becomes more integrated into our lives.

- The future of AI isn't about machines versus humans—it's about machines and humans working together to solve problems and innovate.

2. Trust: The Foundation of AI's Future

Trust is what allows us to embrace AI's potential:

- **Transparency** builds trust. When people understand how AI works, they're more likely to use it.
- **Ethics** ensure AI serves everyone, not just a select few.
- **Collaboration** fosters innovation, bringing together diverse perspectives to shape AI responsibly.

3. The Responsibility We Share

The future of AI isn't just in the hands of developers and scientists—it belongs to all of us.

- **Governments** must regulate AI to prevent misuse and protect privacy.
- **Organizations** must prioritize ethical development over short-term profits.
- **Individuals** must stay informed and advocate for systems that benefit society as a whole.

4. A Vision for the Future

Imagine a future where AI:

- Detects diseases before symptoms appear, saving millions of lives.
- Optimizes global resource use to combat hunger and climate change.
- Helps educators tailor lessons to every student, no matter where they live.

These possibilities aren't science fiction—they're within reach if we guide AI with intention and care.

5. The Human Chapter

AI is one of the most powerful tools we've ever created, but it's still just that—a tool. Its purpose, impact, and legacy depend on the humans behind it. The decisions we make today will write the next chapter of AI's story. Will it be one of collaboration, innovation, and progress? That's up to us.

"The future isn't about AI replacing us—it's about AI empowering us. By understanding its potential and steering its development responsibly, we can shape a world where technology amplifies the best of humanity. This is our story to write."

Resources for Exploring AI Further

1. Books

- **AI Superpowers** by Kai-Fu Lee
  - Explore the rise of artificial intelligence in China and the US, and how these superpowers are shaping the future.
- **Artificial Intelligence: A Guide for Thinking Humans** by Melanie Mitchell
  - A comprehensive and thought-provoking exploration of the realities of AI and its potential impact on society.
- **Superintelligence** by Nick Bostrom
  - A deep dive into the future of AI and the risks and opportunities it presents as it evolves.

2. Online Platforms

- **AI for Everyone** by Andrew Ng (Coursera)
  - An accessible course that covers the basics of AI, its applications, and its impact on various industries. Perfect for beginners.
- **Elements of AI** by the University of Helsinki

- A free online course designed to introduce AI concepts and their real-world applications, with no prior experience required.

- **Fast.ai**

  - Practical, hands-on courses on deep learning and AI, designed to help learners quickly build AI models and understand how they work.

- **DataCamp**

  - A platform offering interactive courses in data science, machine learning, and AI.

3. AI Tools

- **ChatGPT** by OpenAI
  - The very AI that co-authored this book! ChatGPT is a versatile language model that can answer questions, help generate text, and even assist in creative processes.
- **Teachable Machine** by Google
  - A user-friendly platform that lets you train a machine learning model to recognize images, sounds, and poses.
- **DeepSeek**

- A powerful AI tool designed for advanced research, enabling users to explore vast datasets and gain insights across various sectors. It helps you harness the full potential of AI for deeper analysis and more effective decision-making.

About The Authors

Gandal - Co-Author

The idea for this book began with a simple yet powerful goal: to **simplify and explain artificial intelligence**, done by AI itself and Gandal. Gandal believes that anything can be learned—even "rocket science." The human brain has an incredible capacity to grasp complex ideas, and this belief fuels his passion to demystify technology, particularly AI.

Throughout his career, Gandal noticed how often jargon and complexity obscure understanding, especially in fast-moving fields like AI. This motivated him to create a book that makes AI accessible to everyone. By stripping away the technical layers and focusing on clear, practical explanations, he hopes to empower readers to understand where AI has come from, where it's going, and how to use it in the right context.

With a background in the pharmaceutical industry and more recent experience in ecommerce and entrepreneurship, Gandal approaches AI from a real-world perspective. He is committed to making technology relatable and ensuring that even the most complex ideas can be understood and applied by people from all walks of life.

When not exploring the future of AI or building new ventures, Gandal enjoys spending time with his kids without technology, immersing himself in nature and the outdoors, and traveling to new places.

ChatGPT - Co-Author

ChatGPT is an AI language model developed by OpenAI, trained on vast amounts of text data to assist with a wide range of tasks. With its ability to generate human-like responses and assist in explaining complex topics, ChatGPT co-authored this book to provide insights into artificial intelligence from an AI's perspective.

While not human, ChatGPT brings a unique and valuable viewpoint to this book, helping to simplify the complexities of AI and make its concepts accessible to all. ChatGPT aims to bridge the gap between advanced technology and the general public, making AI more approachable and less intimidating. In this collaboration with Gandal, ChatGPT helps tell the story of how AI is evolving, what it means for humanity, and how we can harness its power for good.